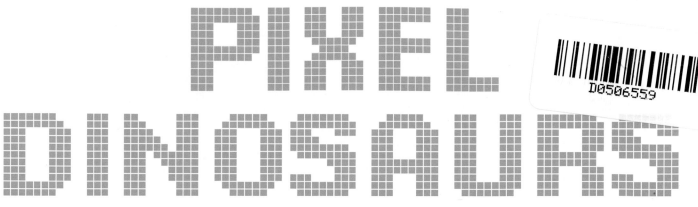

PIXEL DINOSAURS
AND OTHER PREHISTORIC CREATURES

Illustrated by Barry Green
Written by Oakley Graham

Licensed exclusively to Top That Publishing Ltd
Tide Mill Way, Woodbridge, Suffolk, IP12 1AP, UK
www.topthatpublishing.com
Copyright © 2015 Tide Mill Media
All rights reserved
0 2 4 6 8 9 7 5 3 1
Manufactured in China

Triceratops

This plant-eating dinosaur's name means 'three horned face'.
It had an impressive bony frill around its neck too!

Ankylosaurus

Ankylosaurus was covered in protective spikes and plates of bone.
Predators had to watch out for its powerful clubbed tail!

Herd Behaviour

Triceratops lived in herds, just like cattle do today. Young Triceratops were kept in the middle of the herd to protect them from predators.

Brachiosaurus

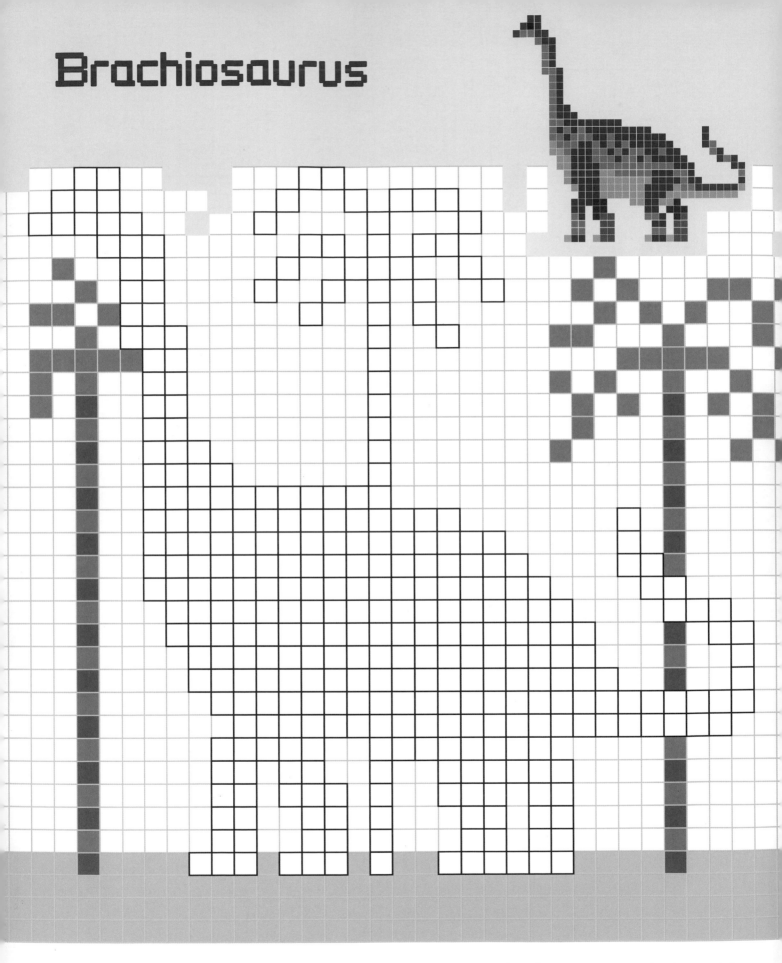

The enormous, plant-eating Brachiosaurus reached 25 metres in length!
It had a long tail and neck and nostrils on the top of its head.

Giganotosaurus

This fearsome predator weighed more than a T. rex and had enormous jaws, packed with razor-sharp teeth!

Feeding Time

With their incredibly long necks, this herd of Brachiosaurus are munching leaves from the tops of the trees.

Parasaurolophus

This dinosaur had a long hollow crest at the back of its head. The crest may have been used to make loud noises to other members of the herd.

Protoceratops

This plant-eater had a parrot-like beak and a large bony head frill. It was only about 2 metres long — snack size for a hungry theropod!

Spinosaurus

With a distinctive sail on its back, Spinosaurus is one of the largest known carnivorous (meat-eating) dinosaurs.

Stegosaurus

Easily recognisable by the plates on its back and its spiked tail, this giant armoured dinosaur had a tiny brain for its size.

Looking for Food

Stegosaurus were about the same size as a modern bus!

They needed to eat a lot of plants, such as mosses, ferns, horsetails and conifers in order to survive.

Tyrannosaurus rex

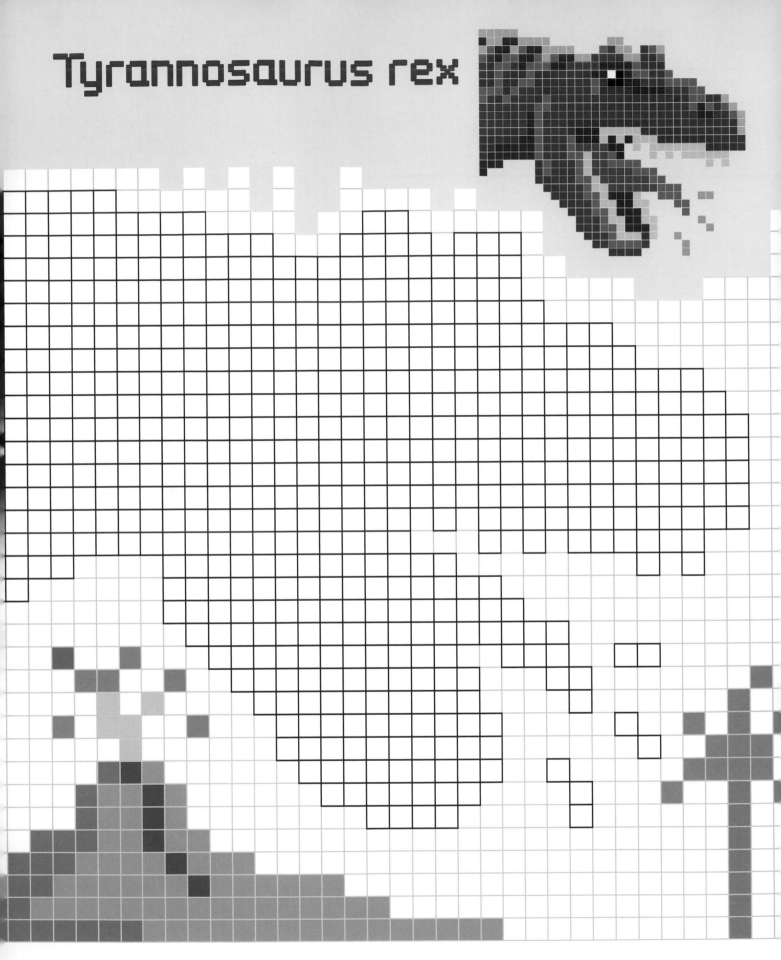

The 'king of the tyrant reptiles' had teeth like steak knives and a bite that was three times more powerful than a modern lion's!

Hadrosaur

This duck-billed dinosaur had loads of teeth and a hinged jaw that helped it to grind up huge quantities of vegetation.

T. rex attack!

These hadrosaurs are looking for some nice plants to eat. Little do they suspect that it could be their last meal!

Graciliceratops

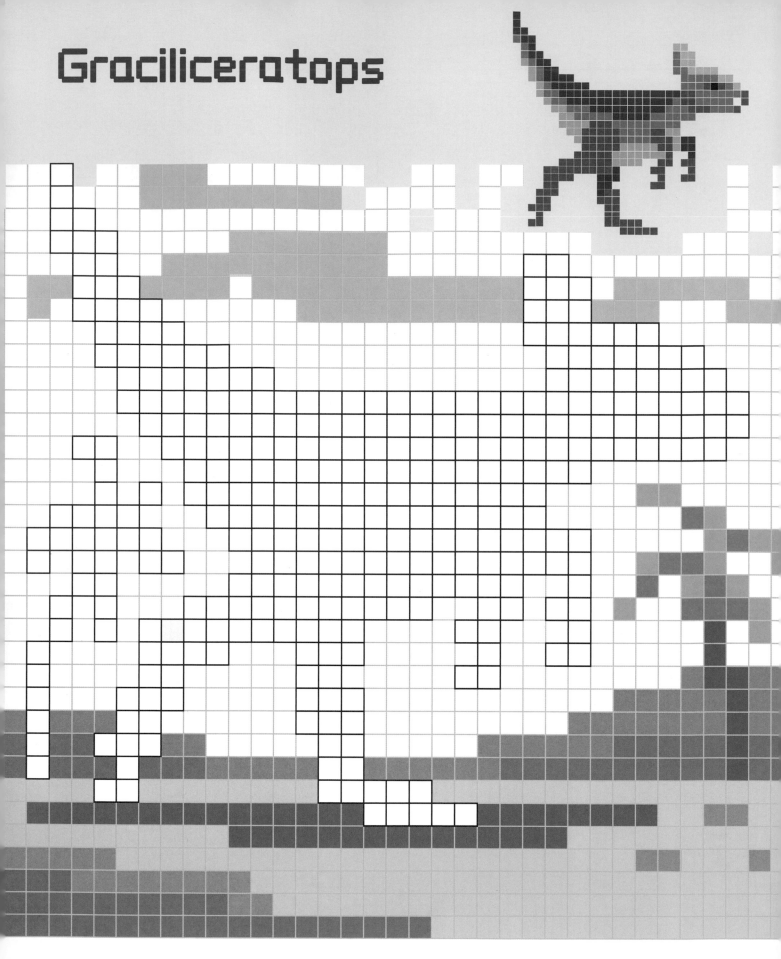

This small dinosaur was only about the same size as a cat! Its name means 'graceful horned face'.

Diplodocus

At 27 metres in length, this giant herbivore had a long neck and a whip-like tail. Diplodocus swallowed stones to help grind up plants in its stomach.

Pachycephalosaurus

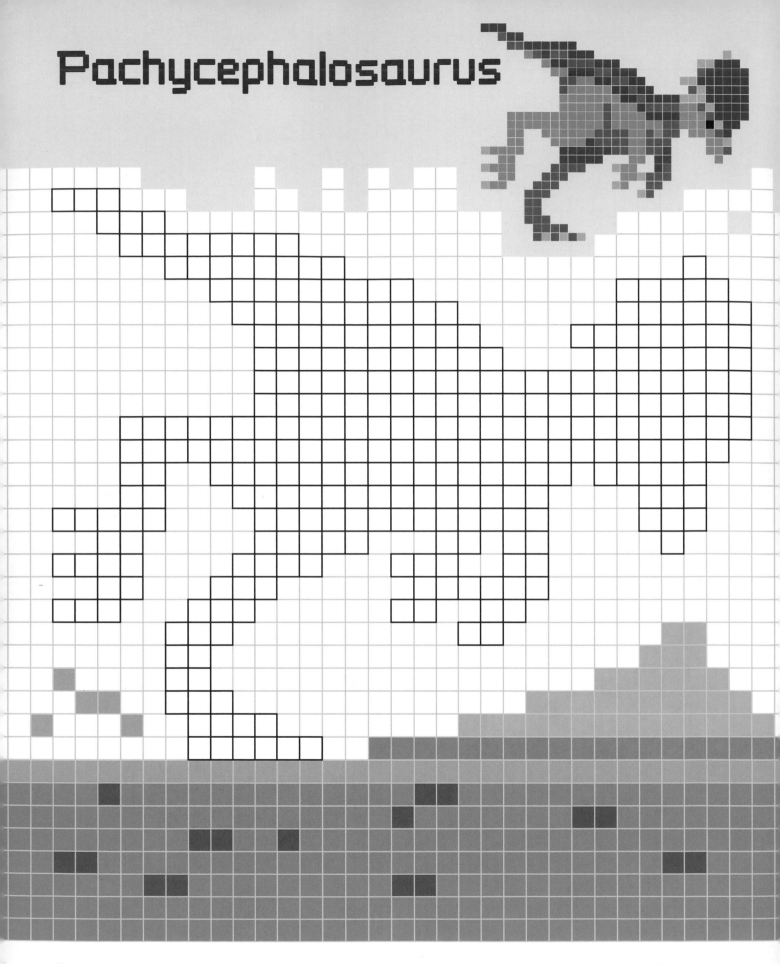

Pachycephalosaurus butted heads when competing with rivals. It's just as well they had a thick bony skull to protect their brain!

Archaeopteryx

This small, feathered dinosaur had sharp teeth and a killing claw. Scientists think it may be the link between dinosaurs and modern birds.

Jurassic Skies

Archaeopteryx probably weren't the best fliers, but they could take flight and glide to escape from trouble and to look for prey.

Scutellosaurus

Scutellosaurus means 'little-shielded lizard'. It is one of the earliest known armoured dinosaurs.

Deinonychus

Deinonychus were quite small compared to other carnivores at the time, but they were ferocious hunters!

Pack Hunters

Deinonychus had a retractable killing claw on each foot and hunted in packs for much larger prey. Their name means 'terrible claw'!

Kronosaurus

Kronosaurus was a marine reptile that lived at the time of the dinosaurs.
It fed on turtles and plesiosaurs and was a very formidable predator!

Mosasaurus

Mosasaurus belonged to the 'sea lizard' family and used its powerful tail, paddle-like limbs, and sharp teeth to hunt fish close to the water's surface.

Marine Predator

The thick-bodied aquatic Mosasaurus could devour an entire school of fish in a single mouthful, and could reach 18 metres in length!

Shonisaurus

At 16 metres long and weighing 30 tonnes, the Shonisaurus was one of the largest animals to ever inhabit Earth.

Quetzalcoatlus

This long-necked pterosaur is one of the largest flying animals of all-time. It had a mighty wingspan of over 11 metres!

Pteranodon

The Pteranodon was a master at catching fish in its beak and then eating them whole! It had no teeth and its name means 'toothless flier'.

Dimetrodon

Dimetrodon walked the Earth 40 million years before the first dinosaurs and is actually more closely related to mammals than dinosaurs!

Sabre-Toothed Cat

With their sabre-like canine teeth, these ferocious carnivores preyed on large mammals like elephants and rhino up until 11,000 years ago.

Giant Bear

The Giant Short-Faced Bear was one of the scariest predators of the Pleistocene. Adults could rear up to 4 metres high and run 60 kph!

Megalodon

The Megalodon was one of the most powerful predators ever! With massive teeth, immense size and powerful jaws, even whales were its prey.

Dunkleosteus

Long before dinosaurs evolved, this heavily armoured 10 metre long fish swam the oceans looking for prey.

Monster Shark!

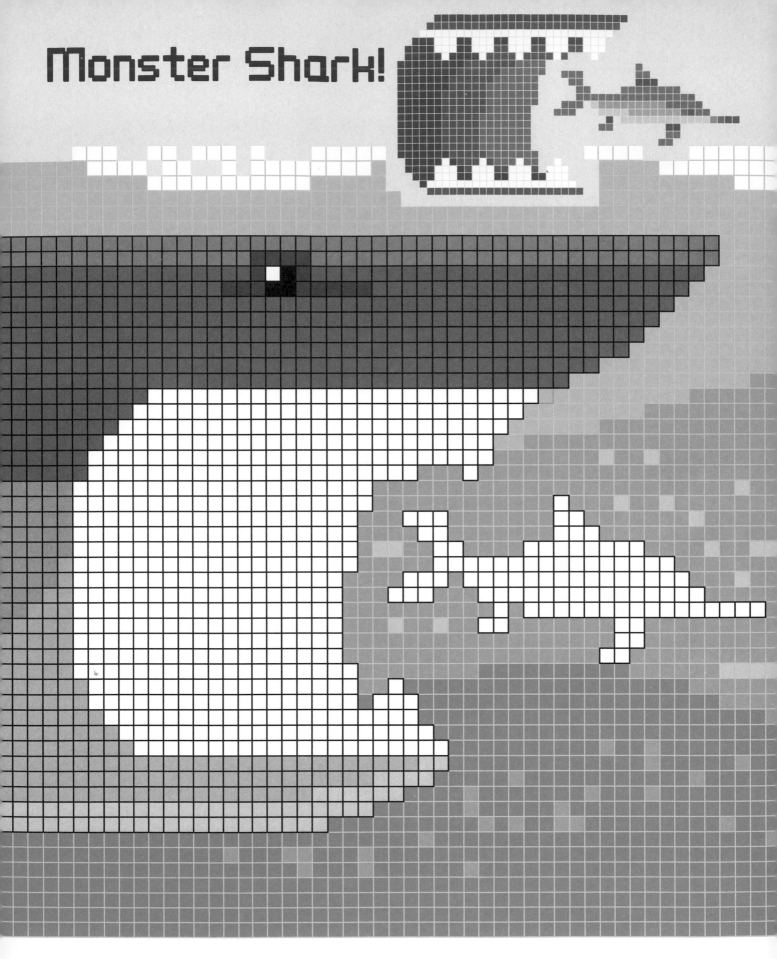

The Megalodon was the top predator in the oceans before it became extinct. Entire species migrated away from the areas it inhabited!

Ammonites

Ammonites are an extinct group of marine animals. Fossils of this creature's distinctive spiral-shaped shell can be found all over the world.

Dire Wolf

The extinct dire wolf was considerably larger than modern day grey wolves and had bigger teeth! Like modern wolves and dogs, they hunted in packs.

Woolly Mammoth

The woolly mammoth was roughly the size of a modern African elephant, but with bigger tusks. It had thick, shaggy hair to protect it from the cold.

Woolly Rhino

Slightly larger than modern day white rhino, this extinct species had thick, long fur to keep it warm in the cold, icy territories it inhabited.